For all the Vestibular Warriors in the universe-
thank you for the inspiration and kindness
that gave me the courage to tell my story.

Keep following the light within you…

UNCOVERING BLISS

© 2019 by Emily Englert
All rights reserved. No part of this document may be reproduced or transmitted in any form or by any means, electronic, mechanical, photocopying, recording, or otherwise, without prior written permission of Emily Englert.

chapters

heart & soul

life behind my window

reflection

showing up

the beginning

anxiety

attack

wellness

doctors, doctors, doctors

my holistic toolkit

motherhood

looking forward

nourish

uncovering me

the comeback

following the light

Em's wellness resources

books & music

references

about the author

In my mind, I separated myself from the vestibular stuff. It was a part of me, but not all of me and it certainly couldn't define me…unless I let it.

heart & soul

I knew I wanted to write a book years before I uncovered what it would be about. I created a health and wellness blog in 2013 sharing my day-to-day life as a plant-based eater, runner, and later my pregnancies and becoming a mother. That little space was my outlet to express myself and connect with others passionate about wellness and would become my training for launching my second website *Bliss Out* (www.bliss-out.co) in 2018. I was sitting on the family room floor of my then-home with headphones on listening to music and letting my mind wander. That is what most of my conversations with the universe look like. The holiday lights were twinkling in the background when the idea of creating a holistic wellness space came to me. What followed was a rush of ideas about the happy wellness hub that I would create. I spent hours, days and weeks writing and designing my website, compiling the details of the holistic toolkit, diet and mindset that had played a huge role in my healing, and eventually thriving with a vestibular condition. The process of writing my e-book *Vestibular Warrior*, which lives on my website, only ignited my ambition to put my story into an actual book, with a concentrated focus on the mind and body experience.

Writing is the perfect medium for sharing stories that are harder to tell through the spoken word. This was especially true for me when I was in the messy middle of a health crisis where I couldn't make sense of how I had even fallen into the chaotic storm or if an exit existed. During that period, it felt impossible to articulate into words how I was feeling. It wasn't that I didn't want to, at that time I truly did not know how to.

This book is to bring a voice to a time when I felt like I'd lost mine. It's also to be a voice for so many who deserve to be heard.

In the beginning I had no idea what had happened to me on that October day. I never could have predicted how a vestibular condition would interject itself into my life and test my mental strength, pushing my edge at every turn. I had no idea that vestibular conditions even existed, and I certainly didn't know that I could be completely lost in a vicious migraine cycle. In the throes of the confusion, I felt like I was trapped in an ungrounded body yet disconnected from it at the same time, mentally drained, scared, sad, determined to find my way out but defeated all at once. Until I was stuck living and breathing it every moment, I never would have understood what it felt like. The raw and silent mind and body experiences and the day-to-day moments make up the foundation of this book.

My heart tells me that I must share my story so that others on a similar trail know that they are not alone. My mind imagines a movement of us taking ownership of our wellness. My soul knows that we are meant to thrive in this human-experience.

I made the decision to share my story to divulge everything that once felt broken and to create a path for others who are battling something that feels overwhelmingly heavy and offer light and love in the universe. I want to expose the mind and body events that took place when my world was flipped upside down. I also feel the need to reveal that there was a bright light of hope in the dark tunnel and the potential for happiness and joy along the path. I so desperately wanted someone who had been in my shoes (or even a similar pair) to tell me that they had made it through. In this book, I tell the story and offer the support that I needed to hear. I share moments of the unrelenting grind of each day and what it took to keep pushing through that darkness. Most importantly, I unfold my journey through the nightmare and how following the light within me became my guide.

There was a time when I felt alone in my battle. Vestibular conditions can be painfully isolating because feeling understood is no simple task and describing the symptoms is not an easy chore. I didn't have the energy to even attempt to convey in the hardest moments how awful it felt, and so I was quiet. Most of the people in my life had no idea what I was going through. However, I now know that I am not alone and over the last few years I have connected with incredible Vestibular Warriors (as I like to call them) who are living with vestibular conditions. People reach out to me just wanting to be understood. I recognize that feeling so intimately. When I hear their voice, it's like my own. Symptoms are confusing and complicated (that's probably an understatement) and treatments vary but when it comes to healing the heartbreak and pain, I think that we understand each other and can relate to one another on the muddy trail. We are simultaneously walking trails that are intertwined and when our paths cross, it's a sigh of relief to find that someone else is also out there. These connections have been wonderfully helpful in my learning about vestibular conditions and migraines, supporting my mind and body in healing, and moving forward with my life in a direction of my choosing. I know that there are so many inspiring stories out there and we simply do not always hear about them since those people are out enjoying their lives, because they did find the light in the tunnel.

The specifics of my getting hit with a vestibular condition are not unique; although, they certainly were to me on that autumn day that will forever be in my memory. This undertaking of telling my story is so that anyone sinking in the darkness of a vestibular something (my term to encompass the broadness of vestibular conditions), battling an endless migraine cycle, or lost in some other fellow health crisis, is presented with a gift of hope and resilience. I think this often becomes a crucial piece to the puzzle of taking ownership of our health and making shifts towards glowing wellness. We must believe that we can make an impact on our health and then take the steps to make it happen, often on an unfamiliar path.

If you are someone lost in a vestibular something, migraine abyss or parallel health crisis, my heart goes out to you. Please know that you are not alone on the trail and there is a community of people fighting to take back their health and live an abundant life. There may be parts of my story that you understand completely because you've been on a similar path. You may have had moments when you felt so out of control of what was happening to your mind and body that you felt entirely powerless. However, what I hope that you've discovered is that you are not defenseless. You are magnificent. I know this because just the fact that you are reading this book means you care big. I believe that there is a world of opportunity to support our health and I will continue to explore and learn, and I hope that you'll join me. My wish is that your soul is ignited to campaign for your health as you navigate the bumpy trail, because you are helping not only yourself but so many others along the way.

On the other hand, if you are someone that has a friend, child, partner, coworker or loved one in your life in a health crisis, thank you for caring and for having the heart to listen to them. This may be a trying time for you as well and I applaud you for just picking up my book. Keep in mind that there are a variety of vestibular conditions as well as forms of migraines. Unfortunately, there is a lot of misdiagnosis and no two individuals' experiences are identical even within the same diagnosis. The symptoms may not be exactly the same but there may be great resemblance. Describing what a vestibular condition feels like can be as hard as describing the taste of water. It's only in retrospect that words have come to me much easier. My silence was a coping mechanism to maintain my calm in the mayhem. The kindest thing that anyone ever did for me was acknowledge that I was scared and lost and tell me that they were there for me. I didn't need to convince or prove how I felt or make sense of it. Because you're reading my story, I know that you've got a loving heart and that person in your life is lucky to have you.

You will notice that I share some of the details of the holistic support, nourishment, mindset and medicine that supported me along the way. I also recount experiences with doctors in western and alternative approaches. Please know that this is just *my* story told through *my* lens. My battle opened my soul until all that was left was me: raw, real and no longer wanting to hide. Everything I communicate here comes from a very heartfelt place because my lifestyle has helped create the sustenance for my happy soul. I give an account of various aspects of my experiences because they play an important part in my life. Everything that I share is personal to me and my experiences. I am not a doctor or a registered dietician and nothing I share here is meant as a cure or diagnosis. I'm a Vestibular Warrior, Health Advocate, a student of holistic nutrition, and a believer in owning my wellness. I will always encourage you to advocate for yourself and your health, do your own research and constantly ask questions. If you're not happy with the answers you're finding, keep searching.

Most of this book was written from my Seattle home. I'd plug in my headphones, look out at the city lights, and just let the words flow. It became a necessity for me to write, almost as a way of releasing the words and setting myself free. My story ebbs and flows and there's no true cause-effect type pattern. That would simplify something that was much more muddled. Sometimes I just had to sit and uncover memories that I had done a good job burying. What I learned through the process is that I was never really broken (but it completely felt that way at one point), rather I was evolving. I am overflowing with love and light and that is what fueled me to write this book. It's my heart and soul transformed into the words, thoughts and feelings that decorated the journey.

Thank you for reading my story and sharing it with others. I'm so happy to have connected with you. I hope that by the end of this book you feel like you have a friend on the trail and someone rooting for you as we venture along.

-Em

life behind my window

Before I broke through the vestibular migraine hold, I felt like I was living behind and viewing my life through a window. This feeling was every moment of every day. My body wasn't allowing me to fully comprehend my surroundings. I could see but it always felt like I was looking through a window, and sometimes not a very clean one. In the beginning it was terrifying. It's every moment and it's a thick glassy window.

I was banging on the window screaming out to the rest of the world and everyone was looking as if to say, "We see you. You look perfectly fine."

Then I'd yell back, "What's with the window?!"

"What window are you talking about?", the world responded.

I'd feel a pang in my heart as it started to sink in. Just because the window was very real for me, in no way meant that the rest of the world could see it. If you have journeyed with a vestibular something, there's a good chance you know exactly what I'm saying.

[Note: VeDA states on its website: "…a large portion of people with migraine often have no accompanying pain, their predominant symptom instead being vertigo (a spinning sensation) or dizziness/ disequilibrium (balance loss), mental confusion, disorientation, dysarthria, visual distortion or altered visual clarity, or extremity paresis. This presentation may result in a visit to the emergency room and extensive laboratory, imaging, and other diagnostic evaluations—often with normal results, which lead to increased confusion and anxiety on the part of the patient."] My understanding of vestibular migraines from the many Vestibular Warriors that I connected with was that I was dealing with a nervous system problem. My eyes fill with tears as I type those symptoms because each one makes my heart hurt. Flashes of memories dance in my head. The dizziness lasted well over a year. The rocking boat feeling lasted a solid nine months. The feeling of unease was a part of me for far too long. My symptoms involved dissociative symptoms, which include derealization (feeling disconnected from your environment) and depersonalization (feeling disconnected from your body), repeated dizziness (or vertigo), nausea and vomiting, balance problems, lightheadedness, photophobia (sensitivity to light), visual issues and feeling unsteady.

Sometimes the window that I looked through would be super clean and I would almost think it wasn't there but then out of nowhere the smudge would return and my heart would sink.

I just had that thing cleaned, what happened!? This window stuff sounds sort of trippy, right? Yeah, that's my vestibular stuff for you, only there's no party and no one is on the dance floor, and it's more like a bad dream that doesn't quit.

I learned to live from behind this figurative window. No one else could see it, so it was just a matter of building up my confidence so that I could do everything I once did but this time from behind my window. In time, I did just that. Everything I learned to do from behind my window only empowered me on my journey of healing. I went to work, was a nurturing and caring mother to two little boys, I cooked meals, just simply showed up, found the power in meditation, and eventually found myself running the trails again and finding everything I felt I'd lost- all from behind my window.

I created a beautiful life behind my window and developed a mindset that I could do anything even with my window. That's when something magical happened.

Around fifteen months in with symptoms all day, every day to varying degrees, I started to notice that my window was slightly open. The first time I noticed it, what I felt was pure bliss. I hadn't seen life without my window in what felt like an eternity, and I had started to forget what life looked like without it. I didn't know whether to sob happy tears or scream, or tell everyone in a one-mile radius, so I just danced in the kitchen (more on that later).

In the beginning the window didn't stay open completely. It would open, and stormy days would blow it a bit closed. Eventually, my toolkit kept it open (we'll talk about that too).

Every day I stop to look at the world longer than I ever did before, because with vestibular stuff there's a before and after, and my aftermath started out a thick smudgy window with lots of rainy days. Over time, with persistence, putting self-care first, nourishing my body, refusing to look backwards and finding a doctor who understood, I stepped through. I thank the universe for giving me the support to shatter my window. These days I rarely have moments behind it. It happens here and there, and it again ignites a new sense of gratitude when I find my balance.

If you're behind your window, I can step alongside you and point towards the direction of hope. I want you to know that you're not alone even though I know behind there it often feels so isolating. I can only share what has helped me break my window. By sharing, it heals the pieces of me that were wounded as I pounded that window with my fists and eventually found the hammer to finish the job. By telling my story all the parts that were bruised as I stepped through the shattered glass are exposed.

For a while I wanted to be all perfectly put together because I figured then the world would never know about my secret window. Now I want to show the pieces of broken glass, so others know that it's possible to step through. It's not an easy journey and it has certainly left its mark, but that broken glass is now an incredible reminder of the power of the human spirit.

reflection

Sometimes I just really needed to feel how this experience was shaping me. I had to truly unleash all the emotions swirling around in my chest and acknowledge it. I still feel like my heart is processing bits and pieces.

If you had asked me how I was doing three years ago, I would have lied to you. Not because I didn't think you cared to know the truth but because I didn't know mine. I would have told you that all is well as I stood there disconnected from my own body, floating away, scared beyond words, mental fatigue sucking my mind, and an empty soul desperate to feel grounded. I wouldn't have been honest because I didn't have the words to tell you how heartbreaking it all was. That my world was full of so much love and beauty, but I couldn't fully experience it because of what was consuming my every thought. I wouldn't have mentioned that I was frightened that this hellish dimension was taking me. My foundation wasn't on solid ground.

I was unknowingly experiencing vestibular migraines.

I remember saying out loud that I'd rather lose my arm than go through this. That's not a fair statement to say and I know that now but in the thick of vestibular symptom hell, I was angry. That anger was just a cover for sadness though. In the darkest moments the derealization was so intense that I felt like I was losing my grip on reality. One of the emotions I tap into most when talking with other Vestibular Warriors is that feeling of desperation. I know that feeling intimately. I have a clear memory of the time that I was driving and felt the anxiety spike. That raging anxiety that warned me the vestibular storm was on the way. I safely pulled over in a parking lot and got out of the car. My world was off kilter and I no longer felt connected to the body that was apparently mine. The tears started falling as I tried to spatially gather my surroundings. All I felt was overwhelming fear and desperation. That is the dark part of the story.

The light part is that I did gather myself even though I was rattled to my core. I showed up that day like nothing had happened and I somehow made it through. Because I did that, I looked desperation in the eye. The fear didn't disappear that day, but it also didn't define me. So, when people ask me about conquering that feeling of despair, I'm honest. Feel it and recognize it but figure out how to walk beside it. The more you walk beside it, the more you'll realize it's slipping behind as you move forward.

As I reflect on the last few years, I'm filled with a deep gratitude, which may seem to conflict with the fact that I've been living with a vestibular something. My reality was altered that Halloween day a few years back. The experience of getting hit with a health thing seemingly out-of-nowhere shifted my world on every level.

There's no going back to the day before it all happened; although, sometimes I wonder about that day. What were my struggles and worries? Did I know what a gift it is to feel grounded and entirely connected to this earthly dimension? What would I have done differently had I known that my world was about to be rocked? The day before "the day it all changed" was a Sunday, so I was getting life ready for the workweek ahead. Even though I do not remember the exact details of that day, I did find a picture that I took of me holding my newborn in a baby carrier on my chest. He's in a tiger costume and I'm smiling looking down at him. I look happy. It's the kind of picture I couldn't bear to look at when I was being bombarded with symptoms. Whatever was going on in my mind that day, I certainly was naïve to the events that would take place the following day.

These days it's hard to remember the "me" before the turning point. In so many ways, I feel like a different person. The trail has given me the opportunity to really get to know myself. To face darkness head on and find the light in the dark at every turn. I've uncovered a resilience that was buried deep within me. I open my eyes in the morning and I look around and take in the pure wonder that I can experience this life. I'm brimming with appreciation for where I am today and on solid ground. I feel like I've traveled to the underworld and back, and parts of my psyche are resistant to even acknowledge where it's been. I constantly catch myself looking around at my surroundings still amazed by how fantastically normal it looks. I thank the universe for giving me the chance to tell my story.

My youngest child was three-months-old and my oldest two-years-old when it hit. They had no idea what was happening to their mother but neither did I. All I knew was that my world was tilted on its axis and I was disconnected from the body I was living in. I went into my version of survival mode immediately. For the first week after it all started, I genuinely thought it would pass. It was just a cold and I'd heard of people dealing with vertigo. Certainly, I'd sleep this off – whatever it was - and be perfectly fine, and soon! The days went by that week and although I was marginally better, I only felt like I was sinking deeper. The dizziness was intense and laying down didn't make it any better. Every movement felt as if I was walking on a trampoline and my eyes didn't want to stay focused. In that first week I fell to pieces contemplating what I should do. I mean, I was just crawling around the house less than forty-eight hours earlier. Spatially, I was a disaster. Nothing looked the same or felt the same as it had just a week ago. Walking felt like a test, as if I'd been dropped into an alternate hellish dimension where every movement was an assault to my system.

I cried in the beginning, mostly from the fear of what was happening and the punishing anxiety that would bring me to the floor. Tears would flow in the silent hours of the night as I rocked my baby to sleep. I have memories of my husband placing our newborn in my arms, so I could nurse him. I remember staring at my baby's perfect face saying a silent thank you that he was with me as a reminder of all that I was fighting for. I remember praying to the universe that I'd come out of this hell. Holding onto the wall as I walked trying to feel grounded but stuck with the constant feeling of being on a moving dock (which will probably forever make my insides turn). It all felt so draining, like I was living in someone else's body. It was every moment of every day with the symptoms persistently crashing my system.

However, although I don't know how, I knew I would get through it. No matter what it took. There simply wasn't any other option than to fight back, and so I put my energy towards healing, which is a daunting task especially when you have no idea what you're healing from.

My experience with a vestibular condition quite literally tossed the balance of my mind and body. I used to say, "Imagine that you're standing on a moving dock and walking on a trampoline and it seems as if you're looking through an almost-blurry window, and there's no relief, anywhere. No one knows you're experiencing this either because you look perfectly fine on the outside. That pretty much sums up how I feel." My heart would sink feeling like I had wasted energy trying to explain myself. It sounded so ridiculous.

    I feel the need to emphasize the absurdity of what it felt like because I know that there are so many people out there trying to make sense of the madness. I receive messages from people relating to how I felt and in search of answers. It made me feel foolish trying to put words to it. I was fighting to stay connected to my life when the darkness was creeping in. The only thing I know now about the beginning is that I was putting one foot in front of the other. I was showing up. When I didn't think I could, I showed up. When it took every ounce of my mental and physical willpower to be present, I showed up. I put on a happy face on the outside, and I fell to pieces behind closed doors. I was in a state of panic but in so many ways I couldn't even admit it in the moment. I was afraid to look it in the eye. I didn't even like looking at myself in the mirror feeling like a shadow of myself.

    I'm on the other side now and I'm in a safe place to explore the darkness, once again, because I know there's a way out.

That's why I'll never be the same, because three years (plus a few months) ago I hadn't been through this. I had never heard of vestibular neuritis, vestibular migraines, or any other vestibular condition. I didn't know that I could feel like a shell of a person living in a body that didn't feel like mine. I didn't know that I could get by regardless of the all-consuming, overwhelming and soul crushing symptoms. But I know now and that can never be taken from me. Because I know, I will pour out the details so that someone sitting in fear is handed a flashlight.

You should know that I made it through the tunnel.

It was a slow and arduous process, but it happened. The other end of the tunnel doesn't look identical for all of us, but I believe there is happiness, love and a bounty of possibility. There's a vast opportunity to elevate our wellness and make strides toward vibrant health. I'm telling you this because I never anticipated any of the events that I share here, and amid it all, there has been so much beauty. I've found myself, and with that my strength, and I know what I'm capable of. So, whatever you're going through, I hope you know that it is ok to be distraught and feel lost but then I want you to pick yourself up and start looking forward. I look towards the direction of where I'm going or where I want to land, and I hold onto the happy moments that make up this life so tight and never let them go.

I'm not at the end of my journey (I don't think we ever are) but I'm at a place where I can shine light to those at the beginning or in the messy middle. The more we shine light, share our stories, and insist on our wellness – even with a vestibular something and beyond – the more these experiences will drive a movement of empowered health and be the best damn thing that ever happened to us.

showing up

I think it's important that I start by shedding some light before diving into the darkness. Not only because I tend to have a glass half-full mindset but also because focusing on the good, even in the most difficult of moments, carried me forward. It would have been simple to get sucked into defeat, even though it felt impossible to return to life. It was a matter of pride on some level. I refused to let my world be taken from me.

Climbing my way through the dark instilled the courage to share my story. I'll never be done learning, but I am at a place of peace with it. I will continue to heal and uncover bliss throughout my life. Most days I feel amazing, as if I never went through the vestibular stuff at all, but of course the mind does not forget. I do not think there's any way of getting hit with a health thing and traveling along unscathed. Losing all sense of control created a sort of unraveling of my layers. It felt like I was stripping down to my soul. It wasn't something that an outsider would have any idea of but for me it was earthshaking.

My soul felt lost during the time when I felt like I was living behind and viewing life through my window. I could see that life was there in front of me, but the glass was a barrier almost taunting me. I just couldn't break free. This feeling was every moment of every day. It's bizarre to describe but every time I talk with a fellow Vestibular Warrior (especially about the experience of vestibular migraines), it's understood. When people share with me that they're experiencing derealization or depersonalization, I understand the hurt. It was my worst symptom at the climax. It was the symptom that kept me hostage to the vestibular condition. Simply put, there are no words for it. It was the blackhole that I had to fight to keep climbing out of. I lived on the edge of the blackhole for the better part of a year. I know what it takes to go through the motions in that state.

However, there was a truly fantastic day around fifteen months in that I remember like a scene from a movie. I play it in my head as a reminder of the spark of light that shone within me that day. It's a day that I continually come back to because I started to notice that my window was slightly open. Not so much so that I could step through and run away from the vestibular stuff but enough that I could see life beyond it and stick my hands through. I couldn't step completely out onto the life stage, but I could feel the fresh air cleansing my system.

I realized that the time would come when I'd break free.

I spent a long while dancing in my kitchen that afternoon. My boys were napping, and I couldn't sit still. I felt so happy but struggled to process it. I had spent a long while focusing on just getting by. Stopping to smell the roses (sort of speak) had not been something I'd gotten in the habit of doing. It had been a blur of motions, trudging through mud and making sure I didn't fall, or lose my boots... There wasn't any energy left to look around and take in the beauty. At least that's how it felt.

That afternoon, I danced, laughed and cried happy tears. I felt life in my soul and a hope that would fuel me in the days to come. Many months, long days, and heartbreaking moments would take place before that day of dancing in the kitchen. Days of blindly looking forward not knowing what was happening to my mind and body, tears of frustration over a lost sense of self, anger at the universe, and eventually an understanding that I would be ok.

My mindset would prove to be my superpower. I looked the same on the outside, so the biggest battle would be with myself, and my willingness to keep showing up.

It was all about showing up.

the beginning

Let's rewind time to October 31st a few years back. It's not a day I like to revisit often but I've found that a part of healing, and thriving, is releasing the stuff that weighs me down. I must unshackle the memories I want to forget and the feelings that make me hold my breath. The day that my vestibular something hit was a typical day in every way. It became the Halloween that shook up my world. I had no warning that this event would happen, and I certainly wasn't prepared for it. The details of that day are quite clear; although, I make a point to keep those memories in the back corner of my mind these days. They are a reminder of where I've been but not something I think about often. It feels like a built-in protective mechanism. A way for me to remember what happened but move beyond the fear. As I recount the details, I pause to take a breath. To prepare to open the door and experience that day...

Life was wonderful and full of love with our toddler and newborn baby. I was managing life on little sleep and had that day not turned into the day that rattled my life, I probably wouldn't be able to distinguish it from any other day at that time. But as you can imagine, I remember so many details: Sitting at my desk at work and suddenly everything going sideways; losing my sense of self in a flash; my eyes drifting and forgetting how to focus; and me scared to my core by the fact that I was no longer walking in a grounded state but rather a floatier one.

It was as if I had jumped dimensions. Have you seen the show *Stranger Things* on Netflix? One of the main characters gets stuck in an alternate dimension called the Upside Down. It's a dimension parallel to the human world and it looks like earth but it's devoid of human life, love, happiness and everything magnificent that makes up the human-experience. It's full of fear and darkness and there is no visible exit. The onset of my vestibular something matches that description just right. I say that to add a little humor to the situation but in all honesty, it was alarming.

It was midday and I was sitting in front of my computer at work when in an instant everything shifted. I blinked and suddenly felt off kilter, completely ungrounded and I couldn't focus on the words on the computer screen. My body jumped into panic mode as I stumbled across the office to find my friend to tell her what was happening, already at a loss for words- something that would happen on countless occasions to follow. After talking to my friend, I decided I needed to get an appointment with a doctor in short order. Fortunately, my doctor's office was less than a five-minute drive and out of desperation I pleaded that I needed an appointment immediately.

I remember an hour or so reprieve when I thought the symptoms were just passing through. During that time was when I went to the doctor's office.

At my appointment, I was told that I had an ear infection and given an antihistamine to treat dizziness and nausea. I told the doctor to run several blood tests (for Lyme and any nutritional deficiencies). I could sense that something was wrong, but I rationalized that dizziness was just something that happens to many people when battling a virus. I went back to work and quickly realized that there was no way I was going to be able to complete the workday and got myself home. I do not remember the drive home, but I do remember sitting on my couch silently freaking out. I sat quietly sobbing unable to think through or beyond how I was feeling. My eyes wouldn't focus correctly, and the floor felt tilted, or maybe that was me. It was confusing and distressing.

That October I had returned to work after my maternity leave with my second child and was getting in the swing of things, balancing life with two little ones. When I think back to that time, I would describe my stress level as typical. I was certainly short on sleep but nothing I hadn't experienced during the newborn phase the first time around. That maternity leave had certainly been harder than my first. It was a completely different game caring for a newborn and a toddler. I remember feeling like I had a light case of the baby blues and was happy to be back in the work flow. In the days that preceded "the moment it all changed" I had come down with a cold but did not think anything of it. I assumed my immune system was a little beat up, but I would be just fine. Within a few days I expected to be back to my normal energetic level. I certainly never predicted what happened next or had any knowledge of it.

At some point that day, I had let my husband know I was ill and couldn't get our boys from daycare. He picked them up and I remember them arriving home. It being Halloween night, my oldest was filled with giddy excitement to go out trick-or-treating for the first time. I was determined to be a part of it. This would be the first of countless times that I would put on a happy face when symptoms were attacking my mind and body. I felt detached from the body I was standing it, and my eyes were seeing things a bit skewed. It still didn't cross my mind that it was anything more than cold symptoms though. I had it in my head that I would just persevere through the night and sleep this off. Being so naïve was a gift in a weird way because had I known the battle ahead, I would not have understood it. I did go out trick-or-treating with my boys and it felt terrible. My balance was in disarray, walking felt like a challenge, and being out in the darkness was unsettling. I just kept focusing on the smiling face of my toddler, filling my heart with joy. Tomorrow would be a brand-new day and this absurdity would be over.

The next day was not bright and shiny.

The symptoms had only intensified to the point that walking was no longer an option. I remember crawling out to the family room telling my husband that I couldn't walk because the dizziness was too intense. He was incredibly concerned, and it quickly became known that I was not going to work and would not be any assistance getting our boys to daycare or doing much of anything for that matter. I sat in the recliner as he handed me our newborn, so I could feed him. My surroundings felt sideways, not spinning but skewed. I was no longer on solid ground. The floating dock that I would live on for months and months to follow was in full force. I wanted my eyes to focus so badly. I remember whipping my head back and forth as if to shake it off. It was futile.

A clear memory that often comes to focus in my mind is of me rocking my precious baby concentrating on his face and thinking I must be here for him. My sweet baby boy was staring up at me with a love that would sustain me in a way I had no knowledge of yet.

That first week was a blur of doctors' appointments. I can barely remember the first appointment and I made a second appointment with a different general practitioner a few days later, so there certainly was nothing productive from the first appointment. The second doctor told me that it was possibly something to do with my inner ear. She recommended that I take Sudafed (a decongestant) for a month and see if it got better. If you just cringed thinking that sort of guidance is ludicrous, I hear you. It felt like I was being brushed off. She also lightly stated that the symptoms could last a month. My mind was screaming saying there's no way this could last a month- that was too long to stomach. I only left the appointment feeling worse. However, that doctor did get me an appointment with a physical therapist that day who performed the Epley maneuver on me several times. As you've probably guessed though, it was no help.

During the first week my symptoms were worse and better. I was up and walking by the end of the week but in the new dimension, like I was stuck in a bubble. I could walk in my bubble; however, it certainly felt different. It felt freaking horrific.

The months that followed are a complete haze of doctors' appointments, tears, putting on a strong façade, pretending I was ok but scared that I wasn't.

I'm sharing about the first few months because while I'm much more open about this part of my life now, there was a time that I wasn't…with barely anyone. Only my family and very close friends knew. I told hardly anyone how awful it was.

Why? Well, I was terrified.

Truly admitting it would only solidify that something really was wrong with me. I absolutely knew that things in my body were out of sync because the symptoms were crashing my system without a moment to breathe. Also, I had no idea what was happening to me. No doctor had put a name to it. At this point, no doctor had told me anything more than I had learned on a simple Google search. I was however getting closer to self-diagnosing myself by the countless hours I'd spent searching the internet. I was frantic for answers and I was breaking inside.

At some point in my search and I couldn't tell you exactly when, I stumbled across the term vestibular neuritis. I matched this term with much of what I was experiencing. [Note: VeDA states on its website: "Vestibular neuritis and labyrinthitis are disorders resulting from an infection that inflames the inner ear or the nerves connecting the inner ear to the brain. This inflammation disrupts the transmission of sensory information from the ear to the brain. Vertigo, dizziness, and difficulties with balance, vision, or hearing may result."]

I went deep diving for pictures from the first few months and there exist very few of me; however, there are many of my boys. I can look at the pictures of my boys and know how I was doing that day. In the ones I did find of me, I'm smiling. In a way that makes me both happy and sad, because there was so much happening underneath that appearance. I don't regret not sharing in the beginning, but I know I must now. If there's someone out there drowning in the initial stages of vestibular neuritis, vestibular migraines or another vestibular something, I want them to know that they are not alone. Even more than that, I want them to know that there are things they can do even when they have no diagnosis and no answers.

You're not handed a manual when a vestibular something hits, and my guess is that a great majority of the people who experience a vestibular condition had little to no knowledge about their condition until it took over their life. I don't think I had ever even said the word "vestibular" before it was something I thought about every second.

As a mom of two young children when it hit, I was never off duty. I went back to work (in a corporate environment) just over a week after it all hit. If you're thinking that's insane, I agree. It was indescribably hard every second of every day. It felt like climbing a hill that never relents but I didn't know any other option. At least at that time I didn't believe there was another option. I looked at each day as an obstacle and breathed a sigh of brief relief when I made it through. I do not have the precise words to emphasize the struggle it took early on. In a big way, showing up from the start saved me though. It required me to show up even when it felt impossible. I was going through the motions, and in doing so I built up my confidence slowly but quite effectively. If you show up one hundred days in a row doing something that you didn't think you could do, it starts to sink in that maybe you just can do it.

I don't tap into the feelings I have associated with those early days often. It was during that time that something started to change within me and in ways that I'd never look at life the same. I remember sitting on the floor next to my boys sobbing on the inside but smiling on the outside at the amount of joy I had from watching them play. My mind was distraught by the symptoms – disconnected feelings, brain fog, drifting eyes, anxiety coursing like fire, and feeling as if I was floating, always floating - and my heart was overflowing with love. It was a conflict within me on every level. My mind and body felt like chaos while my heart was brimming with love. I was a shell of a person with a strong heart. That's the feeling I remember so intensely.

The thing about the beginning was that it didn't just feel like the beginning, because I had no idea what the middle or end even looked like. My diagnosis includes vestibular neuritis and vestibular migraines; although, I say that without certainty, because they are words to label symptoms. I've had doctors mention cervicogenic dizziness and Persistent Postural

Perceptual Dizziness (PPPD) as well. I do not dwell on the labels, I focus on my wellness. In the beginning, I needed a whole heck of a lot of wellness.

The first few months were ugly and overwhelming at every turn. I kept going though, so it's a good reminder that beginnings do not dictate the journey or where we're going. They are simply a starting point. I persistently moved through each day regardless of how I felt and fighting every moment somehow knowing I could do it no matter what. I just showed up.

When I felt like I was standing on a moving dock without a moment of relief, I just kept floating.

When the anxiety was coursing through my body like fire, I let it burn.

When I felt off kilter and completely detached from the world, I hiked through the alternate dimension.

All those moments of just showing up created a season of unraveling, and then growth, making it so I could shine brighter after the storm.

anxiety

The anxiety that came with my vestibular condition could, and often did, bring me to my knees. Crumbling on my bedroom floor because it felt so heavy. I'd succumb to a pile on the ground. It was a physical anxiety that felt like it was swimming in my veins. It was animal and rarely felt connected to my mental state. The initial event had set it free in my system. Anxiety isn't even the correct word for it... It was much more a fight-or-flight feeling that was so intense it felt like a tight sweater glued to my body that I couldn't rip off. For the first year, I was its vessel and it danced around as it pleased.

One of my greatest personal accomplishments was learning to power through when my system felt like it was on fire. This took a lot of time and setbacks. It was apparent to me that my vestibular condition was intertwined with the intense anxious feelings and distinguishing the condition from the panic was a fruitless task. The anxiety was extremely demanding. Or was that just the vestibular condition? My point is that it was all mixed together and that's an important piece to remember. Especially because doctors were quick to brush the condition off as anxiety, but I became accustomed to pushing back.

It was insulting when a doctor tried to simply say that I was just dealing with anxiety.

"There's no way this is purely anxiety," I'd say. "It all started the day it hit... I know there's a connection," I'd insist.

Sadly, I've connected with many other Vestibular Warriors who have been told "it's just anxiety" too. I'm here to scream from the top of the mountain that it is much more complicated. I'm also convinced that anyone who experiences a vestibular condition for five minutes would agree with me. The uneasiness and nervousness coursed my system regularly for the first year. It was as if my body was in a constant state of alarm. Panic attacks behind closed doors and then reentering with a smile on my face was the norm. I once had a chiropractor that I highly respect, tell me that my body was in a state of trauma. Those words were comforting because in that moment that is exactly how it felt. This was what trauma felt like. My body was distressed and the heartache that came with it only heighted the panic.

There were several things that I started incorporating into my wellness routine to gain control in this area of my life, which is the foundation of the holistic support I share on my website. None of it was an immediate fix but became a tool to find my calm in the storm. One of those things was finding the power in movement and meditation.

Exercise was not an option in the beginning. I didn't have the energy or physical willpower to do any more each day than get through the motions. Also, movement felt awful. Bending down to pick up laundry took a concerted effort. I had to make sure I didn't whip my head too quickly causing the dizziness to twirl. Just getting through everyday life was hard enough, let alone adding a workout into the mix. It took me over a year to embrace movement again.

Before having kids, I had been an avid runner for years, racing several half marathons and one marathon. I'd get up at the crack of dawn and get in a run before work. I'd share about it on my wellness blog and then carry on with the day. Now, two kids later and a heavy vestibular condition, I needed something much gentler on my body. The desire to run (at this time) was not there. I attended a beginner's yoga class at a local studio. I was nervous going into the class not knowing how my body would handle the flowy movement. I imagined myself reconnecting with my body though. I was ecstatic after that first session. I knew this was something I was going to love. I felt a glimmer of hope flash in my soul. I was ready to take a step into finding ground in my body.

Not too long after that session, I heard Kait Hurley speak on a podcast about her move + meditate method. Once again, I was intrigued and dove right in. Coming out of a particularly awful period with the vestibular stuff, I needed to get my mind in a different space and I longed to feel the high from working out. Running still didn't feel right but Kait's workouts made my soul so happy. Before work I'd wake up and go right to my family room for a move + meditate session. Some days I'd wobble through every single move. It was not easy. I felt entirely ungrounded and unstable but over weeks, and months, of consistently committing to the workouts, I started to feel amazing (not completely symptom free but progress was made). When the anxiousness was painting my body, I sat in the meditation and let it flow. I no longer tried to ignore it but said a bold hello to it. Letting it know that I was here, and it was no longer boss.

Also, as a total bonus, doing the yoga-like workouts made my body leaner and stronger. I had started the workouts for mental support, to feel more balanced in my body, and to combat the migraine episodes, but in turn they helped my entire wellbeing.

My doctor had given me an emergency medicine to take in the event of being truly overwhelmed with the symptoms, but I was resistant to use it. The few times that I did, it didn't provide nearly the relief I craved, and I knew I needed to keep searching. I experimented with many holistic tools to cope with the stress which was truly an expression of the deep-rooted issue.

Yoga, foam rolling, CBD (non-psychoactive), Epsom salt baths, breathing exercises, natural supplements to calm my nervous system (from my holistic doctor) and essential oils (more on that soon) to name a few.

I was diving into restorative exercises and I planned to gradually find my way back on the trails running. When I did get back into running, around the eighteen-month mark, I was stronger and faster than I'd ever been. My soul was reawakening. I felt myself coming back to life. I'd spent so many years just running and it turns out adding in some soothing and high intensity workouts were just what my body was craving.

I can't say enough good things about Kait Hurley's workouts and if you follow me on social media, you've probably noticed my love for them. Today, yoga and meditation remain a staple in my wellness routine. When I feel a spike of fearful tension, you'll quickly find me diffusing essential oils, chugging water and getting my sweat on. It's a way of acknowledging the symptoms but not letting them dictate my day.

I have a memory of a weekend hanging out on the deck of our old house. I was staring up at the trees. My eyes dancing between the leaves as they always did. I noticed the surprise anxiety spike, feeling as if it was swooshing in every crevice of my being without an exit. For whatever reason on that day, I just stayed still and felt it flow. I remember thinking it was the first time that I just let it swirl and I became drenched in its force. I may have stood there ten minutes or an hour, but I remember feeling like I had made huge strides that day. The vestibular whirlwind had flooded my system and I was still standing.

That became the power I found in movement and meditation. No matter how ungrounded I felt, I was still standing. No matter if the meditation felt impossible, I could reenter life afterwards. The anxiety was losing its power and that discovery started to set me free.

attack

It always starts with a rush of unease, an assault to my system that hits without warning.

I've had vestibular migraine spells happen while eating at a restaurant, mid-conversations, on vacation, while driving (luckily that only happened once, and I pulled over quickly) and various other scenarios. Interestingly, some of my first memories of these episodes date back to my twenties; although, they were so brief that I never thought more about them or connected the dots. It's only in hindsight that I can see how they were a preview of what would hit years later. There was a period of a few weeks in my mid-twenties when I remember feeling very disconnected from my body. At the time I was newly vegan and wondered if it was from the transition, so I played around with my diet. I now know that I was experiencing a cycle of silent migraines (no pain) with the awful symptom of derealization. I also remember coming through the fog. I went to bed one night and felt a little bit more present and knew I was coming through the haze.

In another instance in my mid-twenties, I remember being out to dinner with family and friends and suddenly feeling a bit dizzy as if I'd left my body and was looking at it from the outside. It scared me, and I excused myself to go to the restroom to get a grip on what was happening. I returned and finished my dinner which consisted of a veggie burger and sweet potato fries. I remember because I slowly ate my fries trying to bring myself into the moment, which happened within the hour. It was so bizarre at the time and because it didn't happen again (until five years later), I never thought about it.

The episodes following "the day it all changed" were much more intense. There was no ignoring them or distinguishing them from one another, especially in the early months. No matter where an episode happened, the reactionary dread that followed was always the same. It's not a mental stress that hits but rather my nerves screaming, and a full body wash of jitters courses my entire being. Immediately instinctive fear sets in because I know what likely follows. My body is in red alert mode, no longer capable of maintaining its calm.

Sirens are going off and my body is screaming, "Attack!" and my mind is yelling, "Stop!"

The world then goes sideways in a flash.

When the attack hits, I can see but I've entered that alternate dimension (derealization setting in). I'm back behind my window and doing everything I can to fight it. Pounding on the glass but I can't break it. It's a confusing dimension with no visible exit. I know that I'm still here on this earthly plane but simultaneously feel like I'm not here at all. My main goal becomes not to get sucked in…too deep. To keep hold of reality and claw my way out because I know I can. I've been here before. I'm just not sure how long it will take and how dark it'll get before I find the light.

After one attack, I wrote a blog post sharing about the episode:

In the early afternoon, I felt it start. I suddenly was feeling entirely outside of my body as if my mind and body weren't one in the same at all. I fought back as I always do but I knew when it was time to just listen. I got myself home safely. Threw up at a stop light and stumbled inside trying to pay attention to where my feet were stepping. I sobbed into my husband's loving arms that I was having a vestibular migraine attack. My eyes didn't want to focus, and I felt that dizzy awfulness that's pure torture. Sobbing was the release I needed and then I worked to compose myself, climbing under the covers, winter coat and boots still on. I massaged pure basil and peppermint essential oils on my stomach and temples many times over the hour. Slowly, I felt myself find ground and the nausea relenting. I was rattled to the core, but I was ok. My youngest climbed into bed with me and rested on me, and all was right in the world.

The episodes differed in severity and evolved over time. For the first year my symptoms were constant, so it was hard to distinguish ups and downs. I could not separate the vestibular neuritis symptoms from vestibular migraine episodes. It was a mash-up. Also, since I was still up much of the night with my baby, it was challenging to get a grasp on how I was improving. Was this new-mom fatigue, or was this the vestibular stuff? I didn't pay close attention to attacks, or regressions as I called them, and I learned to (more so forced to) just live in a constant state of dizzy uneasiness. As I healed, the attacks became more apparent. I felt the fluctuations between better and worse. I had the sense that I was feeling better and healing from vestibular neuritis (most likely) but something else was at play. My symptoms were waxing and waning, and I could track the ups and downs. At a year in, I was just starting to uncover that I may be dealing with vestibular migraines. I was talking with a fellow mom Vestibular Warrior, telling her my situation. She told me that her symptoms were quite similar and that she had been diagnosed with vestibular migraines. It was one of those lightbulb moments. I hadn't even considered this condition being in the mix during the twelve previous months.

There are many migraine symptoms, and pain, the classic symptom, is just one of them. I didn't experience pain and had no knowledge of the other migraine forms that first year. The term vestibular migraine is purely a sticker in my mind. It's a way for me to describe my experiences but I'd just as easily call it something else. Even when I had been diagnosed with vestibular migraines (over a year and a half in), it didn't change anything other than giving me a title for the storm.

A year in and I was starting to hit moments, hours and days of eighty percent better. I know that percentage is arbitrary to read but I'm throwing it out there simply to show how the attacks impacted that percentage. I'd think I was getting along fine, slowly climbing my mountain to freedom from the vestibular stuff and a boulder would hit me at full speed making me feel like I had dropped back to the bottom. Ok, maybe not all the way to the trailhead, I was good at grabbing branches and rocks along the downfall. Falling back to thirty percent better when I had been at eighty percent took an emotional toll. It felt like defeat and I had to work through that obstacle with every boulder that fell.

During these attacks my symptoms would reappear and intensify. The floating feeling would return, my eyes would drift, the window would be fully present and my anxiety dancing with flames. It would be reminiscent of the first day when everything hit, and that memory tangled with these attacks made me panic that I was somehow starting over.

Connecting with others in online support groups was such a blessing. Without it I never would have communicated with anyone else going through something like I was. At the 365-day mark, I was climbing out of my version of survival mode and on steadier ground. But the attacks, and the idea that they could happen at any moment, had me in an unintentional state of dread. I was sharing my symptoms much more with others in the support groups and I was getting feedback that it sounded like I was dealing with vestibular migraines. A doctor had never spoken these words to me, but my Vestibular Warrior friends had, and without that reassurance I would have been lost.

I purposely didn't write this book in chronological order because that would have been far too simple. As if to say it was a perfect straight line of healing, which is far from the truth. Vestibular migraines took me on a loop where I'd think I had found my way out but really it was just the beginning of another cycle. It was like exiting the trail only to find that I was at the beginning of a brand-new trail and I had no idea what that trail held. Would it be muddy? Would I be able to sprint through it, or would a branch trip me up? Would I see another person along the way? The unpredictability of vestibular migraines was the most troubling part. I assume this is the case for many who deal with migraines. When it started pouring, I grabbed my rain coat, boots, extra socks, and I'd start building my tent in the hopes of protecting myself as much as possible. By that I mean that I turned to my holistic support system, which we're getting to.

I am still exploring the root cause of my vestibular migraines. I rarely get an attack these days and most days I feel spectacular. I listen closely to my body. If I feel it sway here and there, I know it's speaking to me. My last venture included working with a functional neurologist and having my hormone levels tested. The only way to know what's causing the imbalance is to take steps to assess my body. My mission is to know myself so well that I heal myself from the inside out.

Did you hear that universe? I plan to heal myself.

wellness

    Wellness is not a given. Happiness does not just fall into our laps. Finding bliss from within is not effortless. I believe that my health and happiness (aka bliss) that radiates from the soul is everything that makes up this life. It's the sustenance of my being. I also do not believe that I can experience this bliss unless I make choices to create my reality.

    Getting hit with a vestibular condition threatened everything in my world. I think that we all go through life stuff that challenges us to the core and we are forced to face questions that we never thought we'd have to answer. Those experiences test our mental strength in ways that we never experienced, and amongst all that, it gives us a bright opportunity to evaluate everything we are (or aren't) doing to elevate our wellness, uncover true happiness and radiate bliss.

    When the symptoms all came crashing, I imagine it like this: A tall stack of papers (my life) was thrown into the air, and then there was a breeze, and it started to rain. All I could think was this is going to be a colossal mess to clean up.

    Some of the papers were lost in the wind. I'd have to search hard to find those pieces. Some of the papers were destroyed. I'd have to find my confidence and the defining parts of my essence again. The cover page was sopping wet. Man was I going to have to put on a happy face while I cleaned up this monumental mess.

You get how this connects, right? The job felt so huge in the beginning but page by page I would piece it all back together. My wellness, happiness and inner bliss were floating in the wind on those papers but not lost. That's the important part, so read it again if you missed it. Just because those pages felt lost, by no means meant that those pages couldn't be found, or even better, rewritten.

This brings me to one of my favorite songs since I was a kid, *You Gotta Be* by Des'ree (yes, nineties kid here). I just love that song and blasting it as I travel the twists and turns of this life. Des'ree sings, "You gotta be bad, you gotta be bold, you gotta be wiser, you gotta be hard, you gotta be tough, you gotta be stronger, you gotta be cool, you gotta be calm, you gotta stay together…All I know, all I know, love will save the day."

It was time for me to start showing how tough and strong I really was. To do that I needed to give to my self-care… a lot. I'm talking about contributing to my wellness both intentionally and lovingly. This was no small thing. It took major commitment and making lifestyle shifts.

It was trading in convenience for quality of life. It was advocating for myself and not accepting a label to my condition. Instead of giving it a label, I'd name the comeback. Sure, you call yourself vestibular migraines, and I'll call myself Vestibular Warrior.

I continue to explore everything that promotes vibrant health. I'm a huge proponent of holistic wellness but that's because it has set the foundation for where I am today. It was the raincoat, boots and friend for my mind and body to keep trudging through the muck and pick up each piece of paper. To take stock of what was still there and what would need to be redrafted. Rewriting felt messy but I later learned it was an opportunity. The papers were swirling in the wind around me and I could sit there and watch the wreck, or I could stand up, put on a sturdy raincoat and cute rubber boots and start trudging.

For starters, I believe that my plant-based diet, with an emphasis on whole foods, has been the puzzle piece which gave me the chance to be high functioning even when symptoms were crashing my system. However, even with that belief, I questioned my diet numerous times. I wanted to pinpoint the problem so bad. If it had been the way I was eating, I would have been the first to point fingers and I certainly wished I could have in the early days. Man, that would have been so easy. I'm not of the mindset that one way of eating works perfectly for everyone but through my holistic nutrition studies I have been exposed to the nutritional science of a diet focused on plants as the foundation. Following a plant-based diet fuels my wellbeing now and into the future. Given the opportunity in the dark to feel better though, I would have eaten whatever it took to find me again. It could have contradicted every fiber of my being, but those thoughts are indicative of the pain I was experiencing at that time, not of who I am and what I value. I am human after all.

Secondly, having a holistic support system was (and continues to be) a joyful gift that helped support my emotional and physical health in the storm. For me that has been Certified Pure Therapeutic Grade (CPTG) essential oils, supplements (details in *Vestibular Warrior*), craniosacral work, foam rolling, superfood herbs, meditation... the list goes on. I'm all about experimenting and incorporating what works. In time, starting up a workout routine (which, as I mentioned wasn't until over a year in) gave me the room to regain my stability and find ground, once again.

I slowly rewrote how I felt in my body. Like papers floating in the wind that I grabbed and held down with a rock.

Lastly, I continue to dive deeper into the root cause of my vestibular something (and that might just be for another book!).

doctors, doctors, doctors

I had several appointments with doctors practicing western medicine and sought out doctors of an alternative approach. General practitioners, neurologists, ear nose and throat specialists, physical therapists, chiropractors, a naturopath, a holistic doctor, a functional neurologist... There are a few that deserve to be recognized and without them I certainly would have had a lot less hope and would have felt much more alone in the vestibular avalanche. I am going to touch on my experiences with a few doctors. Although it's a piece to my story, I find the need to emphasize how personal of a journey this is. The doctors that I saw were a stepping stone for me to get across the river. I am so thankful for the ones that were willing to help me and worked to uncover the root cause. The doctors that had no help to offer, I'm thankful for them too, because they sparked my fire to figure it out for myself. They solidified my fierce mission to recreate my wellness.

The first doctor I saw was a general practitioner on the day it all hit. As I mentioned, that doctor told me it was an ear infection, sent me home with an antihistamine and ran a few blood tests at my insistence. I saw another general practitioner, and then another a few days later. My symptoms had gone from disconcerting to all-consuming. The second general practitioner told me it probably was an inner ear infection. That was the day that I was sent to a physical therapist who did the Epley maneuver and sent me on my way. I was told to follow-up if I hadn't improved after doing the maneuver for a few weeks.

I thought the doctors would have the answers. I quickly realized that I was finding more information by Googling my symptoms but that simultaneously heightened my fear.

A few months in I saw my first neurologist. I told him every detail. I sat in his office feeling as if I was floating away and off kilter, my eyes working overtime but excited to finally get in with a neurologist. Surely, he would have answers! He told me nothing more than I had learned from my internet searches. I left feeling as if I had taught him something. I know that sounds ridiculous and probably rude given the schooling he'd gone through to get the title he held but that's simply how it felt. I was offered no answers and not even a small piece of advice as to what step I should take next.

I was experiencing a combination of anger and sadness as a response to the lack of help I was receiving. It became very apparent that the knowledge base on vestibular migraines, or vestibular conditions for that matter, was not high (at least by the doctors I saw at that time).

I was given an order for an MRI scan. At the time I was breastfeeding, and I remember feeling so defeated as I dumped the milk I had pumped after the scan as the receptionist had recommended. I reminded myself that I needed to do whatever it took to get back to me. The MRI results came back normal. I was completely fine. That became the line I'd hear from many doctors. "Your tests look completely normal. You're perfectly healthy." Inside my mind I'd respond, "You'd never say that if you felt how I do for five minutes."

My next stop was with an ear, nose and throat specialist. She was stern and told me that I was fine. My ear testing all came back normal. I felt like I was wasting time, but I had to keep at least exploring all avenues that could possibly provide answers. She suggested that I start taking a magnesium supplement. Many months later I saw another specialist at that practice. At this point my symptoms had improved but I was still without a diagnosis, so I figured I'd pick another doctor's brain. He was kind and fielded my many questions. He was leaning towards cervicogenic dizziness and scheduled a test for a VNG and gave me a prescription for another round of vestibular rehabilitation therapy. The VNG testing was miserable to experience, and my results didn't tell the doctor much of anything. I had wanted to go through the testing though as it was a potential opportunity for answers. [Note: VeDA states on its website: "Electronystagmography (ENG) refers to a group of tests or test battery, and uses small electrodes placed over the skin around the eyes during testing. Videonystagmography (VNG) refers to the same test battery run using goggles with video cameras to monitor the eyes. Both the video cameras and the electrodes can measure eye movements to evaluate signs of vestibular dysfunction or neurological problems... ENG/VNG tests are the most common set of tests administered to people with dizziness, vertigo, and/ or imbalance.]

I came home from the vestibular rehabilitation therapy with a bunch of eye exercises. I performed the exercises and I cannot conclusively say how much they helped. I always felt like the issue was that I could act so normal. I could walk the straight lines and pass the testing. I wished there had been a way to show off how off kilter and floaty I felt inside. However, I do think that vestibular rehabilitation therapy is powerful and effective for many with a vestibular condition. It could have made more of an impact than I realized at that time. Just going through life felt like vestibular therapy though.

At a few months in I was learning to exist with the symptoms and it was exhausting. It felt like a chore. If I search around in the corners of my mind, I can dig up memories from that time. Washing bottles at the sink wondering how I made it through the day. I was so tired. The symptoms took every ounce of energy I had (and beyond my threshold) in the early months.

I remember staring at myself in the mirror, not recognizing the woman in the reflection. I felt disconnected from her. Was I even in that body anymore? Would I just drift off? Could a mind disconnect from the body?

As I was feeling as if I was roaming in the dark without answers, I was connecting with others online that were dealing with vestibular conditions. It is something that I will always be thankful for. I could pour out my heart to a stranger with a vestibular something, and they'd just understand me. I knew I wasn't alone. But why were so many of us struggling? Where were the answers? Why were we having such a hard time getting the help that we needed?

In the first six months, I started going to a chiropractor that specialized in craniosacral work. [A note on craniosacral work- Lauren Roxburgh, an A-list bodyworker and wellness expert states in her book ***The Power Source***: "...craniosacral work is actually far more effective when it comes to stress release, because it deals directly with the nervous system, which is the root of all tension and knots. Craniosacral work looks at the body as an energetic entity, decongesting stuck energy and bringing your nervous system into a more relaxed parasympathetic state."]

The first time that I laid down on the chiropractic table, the doctor asked how I was feeling. I told her it felt as if I was in water, just floating away. I think she felt my desperation. She started me on magnesium supplement (and this time I listened) and told me to cut out gluten. No problem there. I went to appointments three days each week for several months. I'd go on my lunch hour and it was a commitment with both my time and money, but I credit it to making me functional during a time that I very easily could have been drowning in symptoms. I relied on these appointments to keep moving forward, to bring me up out of the darkness, and they carried hope.

I think she knew that I felt like I was drowning, and she encouraged me to keep coming back, and for many months I did. I'd walk in the office and she'd take one look at me and tell me she could sense how sideways I felt. It was like she saw my soul and how broken I felt. I used those appointments to gage how I was doing. I'd lay on the table staring up at the ceiling and just in the way my eyes would focus (or more often drift), I could tell where I stood. She'd put her hands on my head and do the craniosacral work. At that time, I really had no idea what she was doing but I believed in her. Some appointments would bring up a lot of emotions. I'd walk away feeling like I was just holding it together. I credit my many sessions with this doctor to gaining some power over the anxiety. I'd feel it coursing my body as she performed the adjustments and I imagined her healing me. That if I just laid on the table, maybe I'd open my eyes and I'd be all better. Of course, that moment didn't occur. It was much, much more gradual.

About a year in, making my appointments became harder. It wasn't as easy to get away from work and the office was on the other side of town. I could have kept going but I felt good enough to stop. Once I was out of the habit, I officially stopped going. Around this time, I did feel better. The first anniversary felt important. The fact that I had shown up every day for a year gave me a burst of pride. Not anything I'd get congratulations for as I was still incredibly private about my vestibular world; I still didn't have the words for it.

I went twenty-one months without a solid diagnosis. I think this is an important piece to hone in on. I did not believe that I needed a diagnosis to support my health. A lot of that stems from my experience with embracing a vegan diet in 2009, and over the initial transition period experiencing the transformation it provided my body physically but also on an energetic level. My point being, I believed from the start that I could have an impact on my wellness.

I believe that all of us should be empowered to influence our health. I wanted to heal myself. I just had no idea what I was healing from. The physical therapist told me that I probably had labyrinthitis. I went home and researched the condition and landed on the fact that it was more likely vestibular neuritis as I hadn't experienced any hearing changes. I would get frustrated with the details thinking, can't someone just get it right?

My worst experience was with a muscle doctor. I couldn't even tell you her official title but her bedside manner left a lot to be desired. Around a year in I was doing more research on the fascia in the body. I knew part of my issues quite possibly could be fascia related and so I was super excited to be getting in with this doctor. I came in geared with knowledge of what she may offer me; trigger point therapy maybe but certainly some help! I had heard she was one of the best. [Note: Fascia is the soft connective tissue that is located just below the skin and it wraps and connects the muscles, bones, nerves, and blood vessels of the body. If this area interests you, I highly recommended checking out Lauren Roxburgh's website and books.]

I wrote out my whole story of getting hit with (probably) vestibular neuritis, which had triggered vestibular migraines. I explained that during some attacks my neck muscles would get so tight that turning my head would be difficult and painful, and how I had intense tension in my upper back, shoulders and neck. I talked about the initial vertigo spell and the unrelenting symptoms that followed. I wanted her to know everything, so she could give me the answer to all my problems.

I remember her entering the room, her nurse following. She looked at me and said something along the lines of she'd never heard of anyone going through what I was dealing with and she had no idea why I had come to her for an appointment. Side note: I've been told that I'm unflappable. Even if there's a storm inside, I can keep my appearance together. Not that day. Something in me unhinged and the tear gates opened. I had too much riding on this appointment and my hopes had been way too high. Exponentially too high. I could barely piece my words together, so through tears I asked her if there was anything she could do. I was a crumbling mess just wanting to be thrown a crumb. She coldly told me no, offered no comfort and told me she'd write me a prescription for a muscle relaxer. I had no intention of taking the medicine and the tears were only falling harder. She walked out the door, no goodbye, while I quietly sobbed. I could tell that her nurse felt awful. I think she was as stunned as I was. The nurse offered me tissues and I said a defeated thank you. Just typing this experience makes me well up with tears. It's not because she didn't help me. It's because she was another human who in my mind should have had some amount of kindness for a person in a rough point with a chronic condition. She could have made my day just by simply saying she couldn't help me but maybe, just maybe, offering me a suggestion. Instead she looked at broken me and kicked the pieces.

I know other Vestibular Warriors have been in similar situations.

I know now experiences like that lead me to where I am today- thriving with a vestibular something and beyond. A huge thanks to that doctor for the kick in the ass to take ownership of my wellness.

I went a long while, close to a year, without seeing another medical doctor. The appointments I went to in the beginning had sucked the inspiration from my heart. They had proved to be punishing to my soul to show up for those appointments. I had gone in naively expecting answers and walked away with more questions. Throughout that year, I dove deeper into a holistic approach. I started to care less about labeling what was going on and just wanting to heal. I started to listen to my body on a deeper level. I woke up in the morning and assessed how I felt. Not just physically, mentally as well. With the vestibular stuff, the physical and mental swirled together, usually without any map to distinguish one from the other.

The holistic doctor I worked with is the one who looked at me as a person and genuinely wanted to help me heal. Labels and diagnoses didn't matter. The greatest gift that I received was that my symptoms were not being questioned. I was able to feel understood and that alone was powerful. This was about deep mind and body healing. He tapped into the emotional side of the condition. The way that past experiences were a part of it. What I was experiencing was made of so many facets and tapping into the deep-rooted emotional component felt like a blessing. That day I was dancing in the kitchen... that was a huge thanks to this doctor. He helped me see life beyond the vestibular stuff while also showing me that I had the power to act. After each appointment I'd leave with a bag of herbal supplements to take and exercises to perform over the next few weeks.

During one of our first appointments he uncovered that oregano may be helpful in my healing. Ironically the week prior I had started applying pure plant oregano essential oil to the bottoms of my feet (diluted with fractionated coconut oil) because I had read about its antiviral, antifungal, and antibacterial properties. I was putting pieces together too and that was empowering. What did I need most at that time? To feel like I had some control. Every step I took forward showed me that this vestibular something didn't own me.

The last doctor on my journey before I fully "came back to life" was a neurologist. By this point I was done telling my story to doctors. I had created a document which time lined the major events and how I was feeling over the course of those twenty-one months. I wrote down things I'd been told and how I was addressing my symptoms. I booked an appointment with this neurologist because I had seen another neurologist a few weeks prior who had performed tests to evaluate autonomic functioning in my body. My test results came back completely normal. He told me that he didn't know much about vestibular migraines (which I had asked questions about), but he knew a neurologist who did, and got me an appointment. I breathed a sigh of relief.

At this point I was ninety percent better in my mind. I'd have stretches of hours and days of feeling so good, so alive…like myself. I'd almost forget about the vestibular stuff but then an attack would hit out of the blue. The symptoms would flood, and it would take days for me to work back to that ninety percent. My hope was that this new neurologist could tackle those attacks.

She read through my timeline and came in with a soft smile. She told me it certainly seemed like vestibular neuritis had hit, which then triggered the cycle of vestibular migraines. She also told me she'd seen many others dealing with vestibular migraines and helped her patients overcome them. I was ready to listen. I knew going into this appointment that the only thing she could offer me would be medication. I had gone twenty-one months unwilling to try a medication and I felt ready as I ever would. I was ready to put the out-of-the-blue attacks behind me, if possible. I had read the book *Heal Your Headache* by David

Buchholz. I felt knowledgeable (enough) on the migraine-preventive medications that might be offered to me. There was one that I was comfortable trying and sure enough that was what she offered. I said a resounding yes.

This was a big decision for me. I didn't want to use a synthetic medicine. I wanted to figure this out for myself. I was determined but I was beat up. My worst attack to date had happened a few weeks prior and my soul ached. It didn't feel like giving up though trying the medication. It felt like I was putting my wellness first. The short story is that the migraine-preventive medication took me from feeling ninety to one-hundred percent, most days. The major change it gave me was that my eyes were seeing the world as they once had. You'll only understand that statement if you've experienced the visual symptoms that often come with vestibular conditions. I had made wonderful strides to crack my window prior to going on the medication, but with its assistance I broke free, no longer viewing life from behind my window. I was out in front of the window and it felt grand.

I stepped through the fog and slammed the window as I passed through, shattering the glass.

That neurologist was kind and she looked me in the eyes and could tell that I had been through a lot. She offered me hope. The goal of the medication would be to break the cycle and then wean off it. It's a year and a half later, and I've only had a few vestibular migraine attacks, all of which I came through within hours. It's been blissful. My heart and soul found life again and it was during this time that I knew I would write this book. I believe the medicine was effective in my case because of everything else I was doing as well. I couldn't quit yoga and meditation, start eating like garbage and chug coffee each morning. While taking the medication, I had to keep up my end of the bargain, which involves my holistic support system.

In recent months I have taken the step to address a possible hormonal component to the migraine puzzle with a functional neurologist. It's another avenue I'm happy to finally be exploring. My symptoms did set in three months postpartum, so it's always been in my mind that hormones could play a role.

As I dive deeper in my holistic nutrition studies, I'm also in a mode of determination. I want to continue to heal. The support of several doctors has gotten me to where I am today, but I know that my lifestyle will determine the future. I feel like I'm only scratching the surface of where this path is taking me. I believe that I am meant to thrive in this life.

I believe that you are meant to thrive, too.

my holistic toolkit

I couldn't write this book and not dedicate well-deserved space to my holistic toolkit of essential oils. It is a cheerful passion of mine that was illuminated and grown through my vestibular something experience. I explored many avenues to unfold what was happening to my body and how I could support my health. I was left with little encouragement from the medical doctors I'd seen, so it gave me a rather hard shove to start doing the work myself. I should explain that I absolutely believe that there are brilliant medical doctors out there. I can only speak to my experience and talking with many other Vestibular Warriors, that there seems to be a lot unknown about vestibular conditions. Deciding on a diagnosis felt like a guessing game. It was a common occurrence that a doctor would offer up medicine for my "vestibular problem", which I think is something that shouldn't be taken so lightly. What about supporting my overall wellness in healing?

I was frustrated that I didn't have holistic support. I wanted to be healing after all. More than that though, I was determined to find it.

During the first year I didn't look at trying medication as an option. It wasn't something I'd entertain. Throwing another variable into the mix, possible side effects and all, just didn't sit right with me. Further complicating the matter was the fact that I had a newborn, so anything I put into my body made him susceptible to it (during the time that I was breastfeeding). My decision about medication wasn't right or wrong. It merely was the decision that I made at that time.

In the December just two months after it all hit, I ordered myself a pretty package of Certified Pure Therapeutic Grade essential oils. My dear friend helped me get started with a basic kit of pure plant oils after I shared with her bits and pieces of my current struggle with a health thing. I bought myself a starter kit of ten essential oils and a diffuser. When the box arrived, I remember the burst of exhilaration I felt. This was a gift to myself, and I would later learn a means for supporting the health of my family as well. I have the picture that I took of myself in front of our Christmas tree holding up the fancy package. I'm the type of person that if I set my mind on something, I will make it happen. I had purchased these oils, spent extra money that we didn't have at that time, so I made it my mission to learn all I could about them. I bought the book *The Essential Life* and started reading and experimenting with my oils, truly not really knowing what I was doing. Rolling oils on my temples and praying to the universe to give me guidance.

Certified Pure Therapeutic Grade essential oils are naturally occurring, volatile aromatic compounds found in the seeds, bark, stems, roots, flowers and other parts of the plant. The distinctive scent from the plant is the essential oil. Its crazy cool, and as you can probably tell, I find it fascinating. I was thrilled to be doing something to elevate my wellness on my terms and to have some sort of control in the storm. That's the feeling that made me dive in deep.

Just having the essential oils close by awakened a spark within me. I now had mind and body support. Plant power! I was breathing in hope and sighing relief. I carried them with me wherever I went. I just kept reading and experimenting with my oils. All day long I was using them.

Having the oils to focus on was a gift in several ways. They became something I focused my attention on other than the vestibular stuff. I was engrossed with helping my body heal. These essential oils became my holistic support system. It was liberating and thrilling taking back bits of power.

Rolling an essential oil on my spine in the morning is much more than simply a means to boost my immune system. It's a statement about taking ownership of my health and being proactive rather than reactive. Every one of my decisions in the beginning with the vestibular stuff felt reactive. Reacting to every symptom, every feeling, every doctor's appointment, every disappointment… I was so over it.

I no longer live in a reactive mode. I'm now very protective of my wellness and operate on the mindset that I can influence my health. That I should be acting to elevate my wellness every single day, because that is how I uncover my bliss. Essential oils grounded that mindset for me.

I'm purposely not going into the specifics of how I used these oils in this book because it's the foundation of what I share on my website. If you are interested in supporting your mind and body in a holistic manner, I want to empower you to take the steps to do so. Especially if a natural toolkit is brand new to you, and a bit too hippie, I want you to dance on the ledge of your comfort zone, and I hope that you're excited! If you're wondering why I made the choice to use only Certified Pure Therapeutic Grade oils, my alignment is based on the quality and sourcing of those oils. It's an unregulated market out there for essential oils and I am unwilling to use anything other than what I trust to be safe and effective. That is at the heart of my decision. Also, I have experienced how having a natural toolkit promotes my glowing wellness. I was sinking in the mud when those oils arrived, but I made the instinctive decision to start sharing essential oils with others and it has become a part of finding myself in the storm and uncovering my bliss.

The first essential oils class that I taught was five months in with the vestibular stuff. I was still feeling like I was floating as I stood up in front of the class going through a slide show that I had spent many hours working on, fighting brain fog, and plagued with anxiety. I was still behind my window. There were close to fifty people there (over the course of a few classes) as I told my story, why I believe in pure plant essential oils and how they can be used in our lives. The interactions I started to have that day because of sharing my story became a light in my life. It still is and will continue to be.

I share much more about pure plant essential oils and how I use them to support my health with a vestibular something and beyond over on my website. I encourage you to visit me there and if you're feeling drawn to the oils, I would love to support you.

Let the good times (or essential oils) roll.

motherhood

The physical therapist that I saw for a few appointments told me that I was lucky to be a parent when it all hit. Her meaning behind the words was that it gave me a strong reason to keep moving forward. She was right. It was a potent fuel to fight for my wellness and be an example that I was proud of for my boys.

My boys were so young when the vestibular stuff hit, so of course they had no true understanding of anything that I was going through. However, my oldest is now five years old and he understands a lot. He's also perceptive in ways that astound me. I have conversations with him now about why I eat the way I do, why I take supplements, why I use essential oils to support my health (and his), why I share my lifestyle with others, and why I think it all matters. He still might not see the bigger picture, but he understands how important it all is. He even understands how passionate I am about creating an empowered movement when it comes to our health.

I agree that I was blessed to be a mother during the vestibular blizzard. At the same time, I wouldn't wish it on any mama. When I talk with other parents in the middle of a vestibular condition, I feel an ache in my heart for them.

My boys were a constant stream of love that was there for me at every turn. Even in the moments when I just wanted to crumble, my baby would cry requiring me to comfort him, or my older son would want to read a book, and I'd be forced to look beyond everything that I was going through. I would focus on their needs, which in turn became a reminder to take care of myself, so I could show up to take care of them. They forced me to push my limit every day. Doing so became my own version of vestibular therapy. Grocery shopping with two little kiddos is often a challenge for parents but add a vestibular condition to the mix, and it's full on battleship. "Ignore the bright lights, focus on my steps, face the crowd, keep the children happy, get the food, and get out. Phew, I made it."

My husband was my rock throughout it all, helping me hold down the pieces of my life as I weathered the storm. Having his love, support and help with our boys at every turn is something I'm eternally grateful for. He never made me explain any of my symptom and although he couldn't understand what it felt like (no one can unless they too live it), he gave me the space to heal. He also gave me the kind but strong nudge to push forward relentlessly.

I had to have big conversations with myself, and often. I would tell myself that I was going to trudge through the mud in my alternate dimension every single day until it got easier. I would speak mantras to myself while rolling essential oils on my wrists.

"You are safe. You are grounded."

Repeatedly saying it until it started to sink in.

"Emily, you will figure this out. You must show up for your boys."

I wanted to breastfeed my baby for the first year of his life like I had with my first child. That decision was taken from me. I didn't feel like I had a choice, but rather that I was working with the choice made for me. When the first general practitioner I saw prescribed me an antihistamine, I was told to dump my milk. I had a minimal stash of breastmilk in the freezer that I relied on during that time for my baby. I didn't want to deal with any other medications because I didn't want to be dumping my milk. Around six months in I was working with the holistic doctor and taking an all-natural herbal remedy to combat what was potentially causing my symptoms. My milk supply dried up during that time.

It's not the way I wanted my story to go, but I was doing everything I needed to for my health. I share this point because

I'm sure there are other mothers who have been in this tough situation.

When I talk with other Vestibular Warriors who are parents and/or were hit with their vestibular something during pregnancy or postpartum, I understand their pain. It's not only for themselves, it's for the life they created and the person they want to be for their children. I think all Vestibular Warriors are superheroes. Mama Vestibular Warriors just hold a special place in my heart.

The greatest thing that I did for myself when it came to motherhood was giving myself a little recognition. Instead of feeling bad for myself that I was dealing with a health thing, I decided that I would use it as an opportunity to be an example. I would show my boys that in life difficult times happen. The magic is in how we hike through those times. Their number one need (aside from survival necessities) was, and is, love. I started to shift my story. I'm a Vestibular Warrior, I'm a mother, and I can give my boys love every single day.

"I am safe. I am grounded. I can provide love."

looking forward

I think the memory of what life was like before the vestibular condition is the hardest part in the beginning. I was grasping for the past and it was slipping through my fingers. Sometimes I imagined that I would wake up and everything would go back to normal. A girl can dream, right?

I never thought about feeling grounded and suddenly all I longed for was to be in the earthly dependable dimension instead of the floaty hellish one I'd been transported to. There was no one in this new dimension telling me what was going on. Why am I here?

I had countless conversations with the universe pleading for insight. I'm the kind of woman who likes to look for signs. I spent hours searching for answers and the universe was kind in many ways. Within a few months I had a better understanding of what was *possibly* happening to me. I had some ideas but confirming the facts was like running through mud. I'd think I was getting somewhere and then unexpectedly sink deeper. What I couldn't see in the beginning, and even when I was lost somewhere in the middle, was that I was covering much more ground than I could understand at that time. I was creating the trail so there weren't any markers for reassurance that I was on the path.

In my opinion, progress is not linear.

While my heart was aching, my mindset was holding me up. When my mind was depleted, my heart stepped up and showed me beauty in this life. Beauty will always exist, but the complexity is that we must be willing to see it.

Learning that I was not alone on this trail; relentless willpower; better days; discovering my confidence; feeling my soul reawaken; connecting; releasing the weight; finding and becoming more myself; walking the trail; looking forward rather than back… it was all part of the journey.

The shift from looking backwards to only forwards was gradual. I didn't know what forward could look like, but I knew how I felt before. I also knew how it felt in the monotonous middle. It was bizarre when I started to forget what "normal" felt like. I think that if you're in the midst of a vestibular something, it becomes easy to question every glitch, every sway, every heightened emotion… Anxiety became a storm, and simple tasks took on a new meaning.

As I started to find a grounded state, I still questioned if this was my normal. Sometimes, I still do. However, I know it doesn't matter so long as I keep uncovering my bliss and keep looking forward. I share the heartbreak of the beginning because it helps me heal and I hope that it helps someone sitting in their beginning. For a while I blocked out the beginning. I simply could not revisit that period if I wanted to progress. Now I'm digging around and for the first time letting myself acknowledge what that time meant for me.

Heartache hurts, and I describe the experience of getting hit with a vestibular condition that way because it hurt my heart. I'm ok with exploring that hurt now because I believe it can be healed. By the way, I believe that you can heal too. I think that it looks different for each of us but just know that you do not have to go it alone.

nourish

While writing this book, I was also studying to become certified as a holistic nutritionist as a gift to myself. I believe in the power of food. It is the essence of our being. It's so much more than just a source of survival. I think of the food I eat as the sustenance of my livelihood and first line of defense. I know that what I eat plays a powerful role in my physical and emotional quality of life and is essential to my wellness.

I'm a plant-based eater but the basis of that is whole, from the earth, real food. I will immediately credit a large part of my ability to heal (and thrive) with a vestibular condition to the way I was eating. In my mind, there's no doubt about it. I know in my soul that it pulled me up and out of the darkness enough so that I had the energy to push forward. How do I know this? All based on how I felt while trudging in the dark, finding the light and confidently walking my path. It's only recently that I dived deeper into the nutritional science of why a plant-based diet is the ticket to vibrant health for us and this planet of ours.

Ask anyone who has embraced a vegan diet (and stuck to it) why they eat the way they do. There's a great big reason. You know that feeling that you get when a good song comes on and you're alone in the kitchen making dinner and you just start dancing? The dancing isn't for anyone but you, and it feels amazing. It's like nothing else in the world matters in those moments and you just feel alive. You're glowing. That's how I describe the gift of a plant-based diet. It gave me my glow (even if I'm the only one who can see it). I believe that diet is an ultra-personal decision. This choice has the power to make huge shifts in our bodies and our world and this is an important conversation and one that I've had with myself many times.

We're going to travel back in time, over ten years ago, so you get to know the girl from my past. Because that younger version of myself was lost when it comes to happiness. Let me be clear that being lost is not a bad thing. In the moment, it certainly creates a lot of uncomfortable feelings but it's a huge occasion to grow. For me, it was the first intense experience of getting to really know myself.

Happiness is an inside job. I've heard that expression many times and it resonates with me. I get that people bring each other happiness and what a beautiful thing that is. I look at my boys and I am overcome with happiness. But there's another component to happiness and that crucial part emanates from within.

In my early twenties, I was trying to find happiness in the wrong places. It started with how I felt about myself on a very deep level. In short, I wasn't a fan of me. I was going through the motions of what I thought should be my life. I was disconnected from myself and I didn't like myself mainly because there was this loud disconnect. I wasn't listening to my heart.

The universe has a funny way of helping us out; although, if often doesn't feel like help. I had a relationship end out of the blue and in a blink, everything changed. I was shattered from the experience (and the circumstances) but it was honestly just what I needed. I clearly wasn't ready to start listening to what my heart was telling me but somewhere deep inside I knew this event was a huge blessing in disguise. I had been trying to make a relationship something that it wasn't. But that was sort of what I was doing with everything else in my life at that time too.

A few months prior I had stumbled across a book that would change my life and my outlook. The book talked about feeling amazing, being kind to my body and bringing good into this world. Things I certainly couldn't relate to at that time but something in my soul stirred. It yearned to feel that type of goodness, and so I read on.

I should mention that from junior year of college until this point I had been bordering the line of an eating disorder. It was very much related to my life at that time, my lack of control and thinking that skinny could mean happy. Years later I would learn that certainly wasn't the case. I remember looking at myself in the mirror one day, my pants were looser than they'd ever been, and the number on the scale was the lowest I'd ever seen, and I was profoundly unhappy. It sunk in.

So that day in the bookstore when I found a book that felt like a bright shiny gift in my lap, I listened. It was the universe telling me to stop pretending, stop being something I wasn't, and start eating to nourish my body and take a new perspective. It would be close to a year later until I would uncover my bliss but there's always a start, and that book, *The Kind Diet* by Alicia Silverstone, was mine.

A year in of embracing a vegan diet and I was still discovering what I could eat. I knew what to eliminate but it would take longer to learn all the wonderful food I could (and should!) incorporate. It would be an adventure and take years to learn the variety of foods that would heal my soul and provide the sustenance for my happy heart. Along this path, I would meet my husband as I was learning and growing more in love with plant-based living, and a few years later have our two boys.

Through creating my website, I knew I wanted to share more about myself. I wanted to be honest about the vestibular stuff so that when people visit my corner of the universe, they can walk away knowing why I care so much about the things I talk about and why I think those things are the ticket to making life changing shifts in our wellness. For me a plant-based diet isn't just a means to feel good (inside and out). There are heartfelt roots beneath it- my story.

Embracing a plant-based diet was the catalyst for so much good in my life. It was the trigger for huge change. It was the first time that I looked at myself with love. Change is powerful *and* hard, and I certainly can attest to that. Learning about a vegan diet at twenty-one set my soul on fire. I look back and think of the broken girl who fought her way out- to become herself. In a similar way that I look back at the woman who fought her way through a vestibular something the last three (plus) years.

A plant-based diet was my fresh start. I had no idea the shift it would create in my life and I'm thankful for it every day. It gave me a new perspective on food as nourishment and at the same time released my mind and body of so much negativity. It quite literally shifted my energy.

However, getting hit with a vestibular condition made me question everything, especially my diet. It may surprise you to learn that I almost threw away everything I believed about a vegan diet. I wanted the answer to healing to be easy. I wanted the fact that I didn't eat foods of animal origin to be the reason I got sick. That's a messed-up thing to think when you're a huge supporter of the cause. I'd judge myself for even thinking it. If my diet was part of the cause, then the answer to all my vestibular problems would have been easy. As I'm sure you've guessed, it wasn't the answer. It was quite the opposite. My diet was the anchor fighting to keep me grounded.

Fast forward to around a year in with the vestibular stuff that still could bring me to my knees pleading with the universe… I felt worlds better and had fought like hell to make the progress I had in that year, but I still felt "off". That's my way of super simplifying it. Although the insane brain fog had lifted, and I no longer felt like I was living on a moving dock, I still felt like I was experiencing life behind a curtain. As if there was a split in the curtain so I could see the cloudless life through the crack and I wanted to sprint through but there was a force holding me back. I would have done just about anything to break free.

I took a questioning look at my vegan diet that had been such a happy thing in my soul and truly my fresh start almost a decade earlier. I even wondered if it could "fix me" if I said goodbye to being vegan. Just writing this feels crazy to me that my mind even went there at that time. I wanted to get better– get back to me. I wished it was the answer.

When dealing with a health thing, it felt like others questioned my diet for me, and for a period, the voices started to penetrate. Ultimately, it made my heart hurt to think that breaking vegan could be the answer (to my vestibular migraines). In time, I stood strong in my stance that my diet – the food that had nourished my mind and body through hell – wasn't faulty. I still had more figuring out to do but crushing the lifestyle that truly sets my soul on fire and has been the source of so much love in my life, was only going to hurt me.

I believe in a plant-based diet with everything that makes up my being. I have uncovered the bliss that comes with fueling my wellness with plant powered foods. I know the glow that comes with it. I also know that it's ok that I had to make that decision to embrace a vegan diet, once again. If you've questioned something incredibly close to your heart, I hear you. I know that you're brave for doing that. In fact, I applaud you because it probably took a lot of courage. Also, I know now that when life gets blurry, it's time to adjust my focus. At the end of the day, I'm vegan not only for myself but for all that's wonderful in this world. The opportunity I had to refine that focus is something I'm grateful for every day.

Diving into my holistic nutrition studies has only solidified my love for a vegan lifestyle. It's a reminder of why I first went vegan a decade ago and why it continues to be such a force in my life. It gives me the opportunity to wake up every morning and do something beautiful for me *and* this planet. This is truly a bigger conversation (and one I'd love to have!) but for this book, I think the most important part is looking at food as medicine. A bowl of oatmeal topped with a splash of oat milk with a sprinkling of blueberries turns into a delicious sight. Deciding to heal myself meant taking responsibility for how I treated my body. This is something that felt all too complicated when my body didn't feel like my own. That disconnection was strong. So, on the days when I wanted to say f*ck it, I sometimes did. I drank the coffee and ate the cake and enjoyed it all. I operate within my vegan framework and that is what works best for me.

There's no perfect diet. I supplement to fill the gaps. It's my choice because it gives me peace of mind that although I may be trying hard to meet my body's needs, I recognize that in times of deep healing I may need assistance. That's not a vegan thing, that's a human thing.

I had many tests run to rule out any nutritional deficiencies. One of the first YouTube videos I stumbled across was of a woman who had similar symptoms to mine and discovered she had a vitamin B12 deficiency. Once she started addressing the deficiency, she felt better. I wished for a deficiency. Remember, this was not my rational brain talking. This was the part of me that wanted a quick fix. I wanted a definitive reason for why I felt off kilter, why I felt disconnected, and why my system felt stuck in fight-or-flight mode.

I've spent the last decade, and more intensely the last three years, approaching food as medicine. The quickest way to change how you feel about yourself and the world that you're a part of, is by looking at your diet. I hate to think that this chapter in any way sounds preachy but when I think of the power of diet, I want to share it with all Vestibular Warriors. An excellent eye-opening book is *How Not to Die: Discover the Foods Scientifically Proven to Prevent and Reverse Disease* by Michael Greger M.D. I say that because then it's no longer a matter of opinion. It's a matter of vibrant health for all of us and this planet. Somewhere deep within my pain, I knew I couldn't contribute to the pain of our environmental state. Foods of animal origin couldn't be the answer to my chronic condition. There was something else at play.

For a period of six months I did follow the migraine diet (read *Heal Your Headache* for the details). I cut many things out of my diet and it was hard. Really hard. I had to get to know what my potential migraine triggers were though, so I stuck to it until I no longer felt the need. I brought back the foods that work for me. I eat bananas every day and never have a burrito without guacamole. I add citrus to my water each morning and I eat dark chocolate most days. I incorporated back organic coffee into my life but after an attack post downing of a cold brew coffee, I said goodbye to it again. I'm sure our relationship (my coffee love) will resolve in time. I listen to my body. I pay close attention to how I feel from the foods I eat. It takes me being very thoughtful and intentional with how I eat. At this point, it doesn't take any extra effort.

The center of my diet is plant-based whole foods and I eat organic as much as possible. I don't eat dairy. I don't eat animals. I try my best to stay away from white sugar. There was a stretch when I didn't have any gluten. That was harder and took much more of an effort on my part. The first week of cutting out white sugar I felt faint-like. My body wanted sugar so bad. Once I got through the initial stage, I leveled out. A bowl of coconut milk ice cream (with no added sugar) topped with blueberries and sunflower seed butter is dreamy. Cutting white sugar was one of the most powerful things I did to feel stable and more grounded. These days I stick to more natural sweeteners like maple syrup and coconut sugar. I'll always be a dessert lover. Living in Seattle, there are vegan desserts decorating the city and I certainly indulge. In deep healing mode though, I didn't.

I hope this conversation gets you thinking about the food you eat. You have the power to create so much change both inside and out.

uncovering me

Three years ago, I would silently wonder when I'd feel like me again. It was the question that coated every other thought throughout the day. It used to be the question I screamed to the universe. The only thing I so desperately wanted.

My mind and body simply felt like a shell. Even though I was showing up, the world couldn't possibly see the real me because that's the impact of my vestibular condition, at least in the beginning. It tore me into pieces that were so scattered that rebuilding felt like an impossible task. My soul, everything that made up me, felt shattered and I had no clue how to fix me, or even what I was fixing for that matter.

When will I feel like me again? This time sobbing to the universe.

I was still in my body going through the motions, yet I felt trapped because my mind was confused and my physical being so off kilter. Every step felt like a stumble and my brain had detached itself, as if I was living outside my body.

Will I ever feel like me again?

Hopeless moments certainly existed.

Universe, I'm listening. What should I do to get back to me?

It started with me getting real with myself. It meant feeling the raw emotions that come with a vestibular something. I cried and felt that release my body needed, and then I let the obnoxious fear just course my system. Over time as I continued to push forward, the fear slowed down. It wasn't keeping up with my speed.

I wanted to pretend that something wasn't wrong with me. That if I just did everything normal in my life and showed up, that somehow this part of me would just go away. That's not how it works. It wasn't until I said a (figurative) hello to the ugly, that I began to stop drowning in it. I could give it all the power by pretending it wasn't taking me down, or I could face it standing tall.

"I see you vestibular something and I know that you are a part of me, but you are not all of me. You do not define me."

Through making that shift, guess what? I found me. But honestly, it turns out that I was here all along. Just because I was in the middle of a chronic condition didn't mean that I no longer existed.

Feeling lost is not the same as actually being lost.

Acknowledging that I live with a vestibular condition is not the same as accepting it.

I can be me and I can fight back- with a vestibular something.

As Sia sings in one of my favorite songs *Angel By The Wings*, "You can do anything."

the comeback

I've wanted to write this chapter since the day I was hit with the vestibular stuff, only I didn't know it quite yet. Here I am, over three years later, and I will boldly say that I have recovered my wellness.

I do feel like I need to explain what that means for me. Coping with and healing from a vestibular condition has been a process, and I continue to elevate my wellness through the lifestyle I embrace. It doesn't mean that I am completely free of symptoms but most of the time, I am. I do not give symptoms much power any more other than as a sign to listen more closely to my body and what it's telling me. I continue to take a holistic approach to my health and I believe that is almost exclusively why I've gotten to where I am today. My comeback involves a nourishing diet, supplements, stress reduction, chiropractic work, craniosacral work, foam rolling, talk therapy, pure essential oils, self-care, yoga, meditation, and a migraine-preventive medicine.

The amazing part about lifestyle shifts is that they are within our power to support the mind and body in healing. I believe in the power of food as medicine and I love my plant-based diet for the life it gives me. I believe in supplements to fill any gaps, essential oils for mind and body support, and movement to strengthen and cleanse my body. I also believe there is a place for western medicine. Each of these components has played a part in my treatment.

Recovery does not have just one meaning. I know that I've arrived because I'm at a place of peace and I will continue to fight towards feeling my absolute best. I haven't figured it all out. Most days I feel wonderful but there are still off moments and days here and there.

I hate vestibular migraines and the chaos they create but they also changed my life in a beautiful way. Battling a chronic invisible condition leaves its mark. I've grown in ways that I'm proud of and I have learned about myself through the process. My vestibular condition inspired me to help others also navigating life with a vestibular something. I'm thankful for that. The more of us that root for each other, advocate for one another and share our experiences, the more of us that will overcome our vestibular somethings. It'll be a memory of what we rose above. The mountain we climbed to see the magnificent view.

I know that I am incredibly lucky to be where I am today. I know that so many others are still trudging through the dark and I hope by sharing an honest account of my thoughts and feelings that decorated my path, it provides a light for them.

I'm a Vestibular Warrior and my vestibular condition gets the credit for that. It's just a chapter of my story. I like to think of it as my fresh beginning. Really rocky start but I'll be the one journeying somewhere much more beautiful.

following the light

Nothing changes if nothing changes. I believe that I can manifest my reality, but I can't stand alongside it, willing things to happen. I must change my energy and focus it in the direction of where I want to go and what I want to create. Let me tell you a story, so you'll understand my point.

My husband and I have dreamed of moving to the Pacific Northwest of the United States for almost a decade. We visited numerous times over the years falling in love time and time again with the energy of Seattle, Washington but we never thought we'd really make it happen. It was a self-limiting belief at the time.

Feeling as if I'd lost my livelihood during the darkness of the vestibular stuff shifted my mindset. It shifted my energy. I realized that if I wanted to make a life change then I had to take the steps to truly make it happen; otherwise, life was going to pass me by. It sounds so cliché but it's terribly true. Another decade (or two or three) could go by, and I could have done nothing as far as following my dreams. It was easy to stay comfortable, but I had spent over 540 days (12,960 hours!) feeling so far from comfortable every moment of every day. I learned to exist without a comfort within my inner being. So, when I was truly starting to feel like myself again, I no longer wanted to just be comfortable. I wanted to uncover my bliss. My heart told me it was time to make the shift.

Deciding to make a cross country move was surreal, exciting, thrilling and scary. There were so many moving pieces- finding jobs, selling our house, downsizing our life, finding a new home, the logistics of moving, and most importantly making sure it was all what was best for us and our boys. It was a process that took the better part of a year and we serendipitously ended up closing on our house in New York State on the day that we left for our cross-country drive. As we were getting on the road, we got the email from our attorney saying that the closing was done. Just like that, we were free. My husband and I looked at each other smiling saying, "We don't own that house anymore!". This is not to say that owning a house or anything like that is bad or wrong, it's freaking amazing. My point is that living a life that feels cluttered with baggage and toxicity is no way to live. The house and a lot of what came with it was our heavy weight, and we wanted out.

Over five days and 50 (plus) hours we drove the vast country and saw so much beauty. We stayed in Best Westerns and similar hotels along the way and our boys thought it was the best thing ever. They'd never been in hotels and they'd jump from bed to bed laughing endlessly at the fun. We had a Thule on our Subaru and towed a 5 x 8 U-Haul behind us holding everything we owned. We had cleaned out so much from the house and the feeling of minimalizing our life felt entirely rejuvenating. It cleared spaces in my mind and body, and it began to rewire my energy.

We only took with us the clothes we planned to wear going forward (no room for extras), the things that we loved, bedroom furniture, the house essentials, and our boys' toys and belongings. In the final weeks and months before the move we donated probably half of our stuff. The crazy part is that we do not miss any of it. I don't even remember most of it, which just goes to show how much it simply was clutter. Through the process I donated at least ten bags of clothes, many, many books, and kitchen items that were collecting dusk. Unloading the baggage made room for a fresh start. It made room for me to uncover my bliss.

I'm not sure that I would have ever had the courage to make the cross-country move had I not gone through everything I've shared in this book. It opened my eyes, so I not only could see but I took a long hard look at my life. It's not an easy thing to do and anyone that's made big life changes knows it's not effortless and often comes with resistance. A comment that stuck with me was when someone said that I was lucky that I could just pick up and move. That really hit me because it wasn't a matter of luck. It was whole-heartedly intentional, and it took putting all our energy and love in the direction that we wanted to go. This task was something that I finetuned during the darker days, always looking and striving to be where my heart and soul would be at peace. Today we look back so thankful that we had the audacity to go for it.

We drove across the country not knowing what our new home looked like other than pictures we'd seen on the internet. Talk about a leap of faith. When we pulled up to it and opened the front door, I knew it was home. When I discovered that we had our own private balcony looking out towards the city, I was elated.

My point in telling this story is that I believe if you want to make changes in your life, you must start by shifting your energy. Follow the light and know that the universe has your back.

I believe that this life is about uncovering bliss. It's a forever journey and at the heart of every decision I make. Although I know I'm not supposed to share this, dating back to as far as I can remember, on every birthday cake of mine after I've blown out the candles I've never wished for anything but happiness (and health as I got older). It doesn't matter what the happiness looks like. I also think it's something that evolves as I do. What bliss looked like to me at five years old is considerably different than my viewpoint a few decades later.

These days I'm continuing to dive deeper into the intricacies of mind and body wellness. After a decade of plant-based eating, lots of reading and educating myself, I'm now studying holistic nutrition simply because I want to be empowered when it comes to my health. I want to help others do the same. Creating our wellbeing should be something we're all authorized to do. It's a path that I'll continue to follow.

This book is not the end of my story, just a chapter really. Maybe even only a blip in the eternal universe scheme of things. We all have chapters that we often do not share. This was one of mine I simply couldn't be silent about.

Wherever my story is finding you, I have a little homework for you. Put your hands on your heart. Feel everything that's happening in your life right now. Let that energy course your system and feel it emanating from deep within. Cry, laugh, whatever you need to do to feel raw unfiltered emotion, or if it doesn't feel right (yet), just feel your breath. Inhale deeply acknowledging with gratitude everything that makes up you, today. Let out your breath and reflect on everything that you've been through. I bet you have a chapter to share, and I hope that you do.

The first time I realized that this vestibular stuff was going to help me become more in tune with myself, more me, more alive and connected to this beautiful life… I held onto that feeling with all my might.

EM'S WELLNESS RESOURCES

Kait Hurley: Move + Meditate® Method

kaithurley.com

Lauren Roxburgh: expert on all things fascia, alignment, movement and foaming rolling

laurenroxburgh.com

Vestibular Disorders Association (VeDA)

vestibular.org

BOOKS & MUSIC

Heal Your Headache by David Buchholz M.D.

The Kind Diet by Alicia Silverstone

The Essential Life by LLC Total Wellness Publishing

How Not to Die: Discover the Foods Scientifically Proven to Prevent and Reverse Disease by Michael Greger M.D.

The Power Source: The Hidden Key to Ignite Your Core, Empower Your Body, Release Stress, and Realign Your Life by Lauren Roxburgh

Spotify Playlist: Bliss Out by Emily Englert

REFERENCES

https://vestibular.org/labyrinthitis-and-vestibular-neuritis

https://vestibular.org/migraine-associated-vertigo-mav

https://vestibular.org/understanding-vestibular-disorder/diagnosis

Hi there!

I'm so happy that you picked up my book. I am overflowing with love and light and that is what fueled me to write this book. It's my heart and soul transformed into the words, thoughts and feelings that decorated a chapter of my life. Writing is the perfect medium for sharing stories that are harder to tell through the spoken word. This was especially true for me when I was in the messy middle of a health crisis (vestibular condition) where I couldn't make sense of how I had even fallen into the chaotic storm or if an exit existed. During that period, it felt impossible to articulate into words how I was feeling. It wasn't that I didn't want to, at that time I truly did not know how to. My mission is to bring a voice to a time when I felt like I'd lost mine. It's also to be a voice for so many who deserve to be heard.

If you enjoyed my book, please pass it along to a fellow Vestibular Warrior.

Also, I'd love for you to explore my website, Bliss Out. Visit **www.bliss-out.co** to find additional resources, happy holistic goodness to elevate your wellness, and connect with me.

Sending love and light your way.

-Em

Lightning Source UK Ltd.
Milton Keynes UK
UKHW011244020320
359621UK00001B/137

9 781714 363698